50 Barbecue Grill Recipes

By: Kelly Johnson

Table of Contents

- Grilled BBQ Chicken
- Classic Grilled Hamburgers
- BBQ Ribs
- Grilled Hot Dogs
- BBQ Pulled Pork Sandwiches
- Grilled Corn on the Cob
- BBQ Chicken Wings
- Grilled Shrimp Skewers
- Grilled Portobello Mushrooms
- BBQ Brisket
- Grilled Pineapple Slices
- BBQ Sausage Links
- Grilled Vegetable Kabobs
- BBQ Tofu Steaks
- Grilled Salmon with Lemon
- BBQ Meatball Skewers
- Grilled Chicken Fajitas

- Grilled Lamb Chops
- BBQ Pork Chops
- Grilled Zucchini and Squash
- BBQ Flatbread Pizzas
- Grilled Steak Tacos
- Grilled Eggplant Rounds
- BBQ Bacon-Wrapped Jalapeños
- Grilled Chicken Drumsticks
- BBQ Turkey Burgers
- Grilled Halloumi Cheese
- BBQ Pork Tenderloin
- Grilled Peach Halves
- BBQ Glazed Meatloaf
- Grilled Romaine Salad
- BBQ Bratwursts
- Grilled Swordfish Steaks
- BBQ Cauliflower Steaks
- Grilled Bacon-Wrapped Asparagus
- BBQ Glazed Tofu Skewers

- Grilled Nachos
- Grilled Avocado Halves
- BBQ Chicken Pizza
- Grilled Stuffed Peppers
- BBQ Chicken Quesadillas
- Grilled Scallops
- BBQ Sweet Potato Slices
- Grilled Cornbread
- BBQ Cheeseburgers
- Grilled Pineapple Chicken
- BBQ Duck Breasts
- Grilled Stuffed Mushrooms
- BBQ Glazed Tempeh
- Grilled Garlic Bread

Grilled BBQ Chicken

Ingredients:

- 4 bone-in chicken thighs or breasts
- 1 cup BBQ sauce
- Salt and pepper
- Olive oil

Instructions:

1. Preheat grill to medium heat.
2. Brush chicken with olive oil, season with salt and pepper.
3. Grill for 5–7 minutes per side, brushing with BBQ sauce during the last few minutes.
4. Cook until internal temperature reaches 165°F.
5. Let rest for 5 minutes before serving.

Classic Grilled Hamburgers

Ingredients:

- 1 lb ground beef (80/20)
- Salt and pepper
- 4 burger buns
- Optional toppings: cheese, lettuce, tomato, pickles, condiments

Instructions:

1. Shape ground beef into 4 patties, season with salt and pepper.
2. Grill over medium-high heat for 3–4 minutes per side for medium doneness.
3. Toast buns if desired, assemble burgers with toppings.

BBQ Ribs

Ingredients:

- 2 racks baby back ribs
- Dry rub (paprika, brown sugar, garlic powder, salt, pepper)
- 1 cup BBQ sauce

Instructions:

1. Rub ribs with dry seasoning and let sit for at least 30 minutes.
2. Grill over indirect heat (low heat) for 2–2.5 hours, turning occasionally.
3. In the last 15 minutes, brush with BBQ sauce and cook over direct heat for a caramelized finish.

Grilled Hot Dogs

Ingredients:

- 8 hot dogs
- 8 buns
- Optional toppings: mustard, ketchup, relish, onions

Instructions:

1. Preheat grill to medium heat.
2. Grill hot dogs for 5–7 minutes, turning often until lightly charred.
3. Toast buns if desired, serve with toppings.

BBQ Pulled Pork Sandwiches

Ingredients:

- 2 lbs pork shoulder
- 1 tbsp paprika
- 1 tbsp brown sugar
- 1 tsp garlic powder
- Salt and pepper
- 1 cup BBQ sauce
- Buns for serving

Instructions:

1. Rub pork with seasonings and slow-cook or smoke at low heat (275°F) for 6–8 hours until tender.
2. Shred pork, mix with BBQ sauce, and serve on buns.

Grilled Corn on the Cob

Ingredients:

- 4 ears corn
- Butter
- Salt

Instructions:

1. Peel back husks (leave attached), remove silk, soak corn in water 10 min.
2. Grill over medium heat for 15–20 minutes, turning occasionally.
3. Peel back husks, brush with butter, and sprinkle with salt.

BBQ Chicken Wings

Ingredients:

- 2 lbs chicken wings
- Salt and pepper
- 1 cup BBQ sauce

Instructions:

1. Season wings with salt and pepper.
2. Grill over medium heat, turning every 5 minutes for about 20–25 minutes.
3. Brush with BBQ sauce during the last 5 minutes.
4. Cook until crispy and caramelized.

Grilled Shrimp Skewers

Ingredients:

- 1 lb large shrimp, peeled and deveined
- 2 tbsp olive oil
- 2 cloves garlic, minced
- Juice of 1 lemon
- Salt and pepper
- Skewers (soaked if wooden)

Instructions:

1. Toss shrimp with oil, garlic, lemon, salt, and pepper.
2. Skewer and grill over medium-high heat for 2–3 minutes per side.
3. Serve with lemon wedges.

Grilled Portobello Mushrooms

Ingredients:

- 4 large portobello caps
- 2 tbsp balsamic vinegar
- 2 tbsp olive oil
- 1 clove garlic, minced
- Salt and pepper

Instructions:

1. Whisk vinegar, oil, garlic, salt, and pepper; brush onto mushrooms.
2. Grill over medium heat for 4–5 minutes per side until tender.
3. Serve as a side or burger alternative.

BBQ Brisket

Ingredients:

- 4–5 lb beef brisket
- 2 tbsp paprika
- 1 tbsp garlic powder
- 1 tbsp onion powder
- 1 tbsp salt
- 1 tsp black pepper
- 1 cup BBQ sauce

Instructions:

1. Combine dry seasonings and rub all over brisket.
2. Let sit at room temp for 1 hour.
3. Preheat grill to 225°F for indirect heat.
4. Smoke or grill brisket for 6–8 hours, adding wood chips if desired.
5. During the last hour, brush with BBQ sauce.
6. Let rest 20 minutes before slicing.

Grilled Pineapple Slices

Ingredients:

- 1 fresh pineapple, peeled, cored, and sliced
- 2 tbsp brown sugar
- 1 tbsp honey (optional)
- 1 tsp cinnamon (optional)

Instructions:

1. Sprinkle pineapple with brown sugar, honey, and cinnamon if using.
2. Grill over medium heat for 3–4 minutes per side until caramelized.
3. Serve warm as a side or dessert.

BBQ Sausage Links

Ingredients:

- 1–2 lbs sausage links (bratwurst, Italian, etc.)
- BBQ sauce (optional)

Instructions:

1. Preheat grill to medium heat.
2. Grill sausages for 10–15 minutes, turning often, until cooked through.
3. Optional: brush with BBQ sauce in the last 5 minutes for extra flavor.

Grilled Vegetable Kabobs

Ingredients:

- Bell peppers, zucchini, mushrooms, onions (cut into chunks)
- 2 tbsp olive oil
- 1 tsp garlic powder
- Salt and pepper
- Wooden skewers (soaked) or metal skewers

Instructions:

1. Toss vegetables with olive oil, garlic powder, salt, and pepper.
2. Thread onto skewers.
3. Grill over medium-high heat for 8–10 minutes, turning occasionally.

BBQ Tofu Steaks

Ingredients:

- 1 block extra-firm tofu, pressed and sliced
- 1/2 cup BBQ sauce
- Olive oil for brushing

Instructions:

1. Brush tofu slices with oil and BBQ sauce.
2. Grill over medium heat for 4–5 minutes per side until slightly crispy and caramelized.
3. Brush with more BBQ sauce before serving.

Grilled Salmon with Lemon

Ingredients:

- 4 salmon fillets
- 1 lemon, thinly sliced
- Salt and pepper
- 1 tbsp olive oil

Instructions:

1. Preheat grill to medium heat.
2. Brush salmon with oil, season with salt and pepper.
3. Place lemon slices on top.
4. Grill skin-side down for 6–8 minutes, or until flaky.

BBQ Meatball Skewers

Ingredients:

- 1 lb cooked meatballs
- 1 cup BBQ sauce
- Skewers

Instructions:

1. Thread meatballs onto skewers.
2. Brush with BBQ sauce.
3. Grill over medium heat for 8–10 minutes, turning and brushing with more sauce.
4. Serve warm with extra sauce.

Grilled Chicken Fajitas

Ingredients:

- 2 chicken breasts, sliced
- 2 bell peppers, sliced
- 1 onion, sliced
- 2 tbsp olive oil
- 1 tsp chili powder, 1 tsp cumin, salt & pepper

Instructions:

1. Toss chicken and vegetables with oil and spices.
2. Grill chicken for 5–7 minutes per side.
3. Grill veggies in a grill basket or foil for 10–12 minutes.
4. Serve in tortillas or lettuce wraps.

Grilled Lamb Chops

Ingredients:

- 4–6 lamb chops
- 2 tbsp olive oil
- 2 cloves garlic, minced
- 1 tbsp rosemary or thyme
- Salt and pepper

Instructions:

1. Marinate lamb with oil, garlic, herbs, salt, and pepper for at least 30 minutes.
2. Grill over medium-high heat for 3–4 minutes per side for medium-rare.
3. Let rest for 5 minutes before serving.

BBQ Pork Chops

Ingredients:

- 4 bone-in pork chops
- Salt and pepper
- 1 cup BBQ sauce

Instructions:

1. Preheat grill to medium-high.
2. Season pork chops with salt and pepper.
3. Grill 4–5 minutes per side.
4. Brush with BBQ sauce and grill 1–2 more minutes per side.
5. Let rest 5 minutes before serving.

Grilled Zucchini and Squash

Ingredients:

- 2 zucchinis, 2 yellow squash (sliced lengthwise)
- 2 tbsp olive oil
- Salt, pepper, garlic powder

Instructions:

1. Toss vegetables with oil and seasonings.
2. Grill over medium heat for 3–4 minutes per side until tender and charred.
3. Serve warm.

BBQ Flatbread Pizzas

Ingredients:

- 2 flatbreads
- 1/2 cup BBQ sauce
- 1 cup cooked shredded chicken
- 1 cup shredded mozzarella
- Red onion slices, cilantro (optional)

Instructions:

1. Preheat grill to medium.
2. Spread BBQ sauce on flatbreads, top with chicken, cheese, and onions.
3. Grill 3–5 minutes with the lid closed until cheese melts.
4. Garnish with cilantro and serve.

Grilled Steak Tacos

Ingredients:

- 1 lb flank or skirt steak
- 1 tbsp olive oil
- 1 tsp cumin, chili powder, garlic powder
- Salt and pepper
- Tortillas, toppings (salsa, onion, lime, cilantro)

Instructions:

1. Rub steak with oil and seasonings.
2. Grill over high heat for 4–5 minutes per side.
3. Rest 5 minutes, then slice thin.
4. Serve in tortillas with toppings.

Grilled Eggplant Rounds

Ingredients:

- 1 large eggplant, sliced into 1/2" rounds
- Olive oil, salt, pepper, Italian herbs

Instructions:

1. Brush slices with oil and seasonings.
2. Grill over medium heat 3–4 minutes per side.
3. Serve as a side or appetizer.

BBQ Bacon-Wrapped Jalapeños

Ingredients:

- 6 jalapeños, halved and deseeded
- 4 oz cream cheese
- 1/2 cup shredded cheddar
- 12 slices bacon
- BBQ sauce

Instructions:

1. Mix cheeses, fill jalapeño halves.
2. Wrap each with bacon, secure with toothpick.
3. Grill over indirect heat 15–20 minutes, brushing with BBQ sauce in final minutes.
4. Serve warm.

Grilled Chicken Drumsticks

Ingredients:

- 8 chicken drumsticks
- Salt, pepper, garlic powder
- 3/4 cup BBQ sauce

Instructions:

1. Preheat grill to medium.
2. Season drumsticks and grill 25–30 minutes, turning frequently.
3. Brush with BBQ sauce in the last 10 minutes.
4. Cook to internal temp of 165°F.

BBQ Turkey Burgers

Ingredients:

- 1 lb ground turkey
- 1/4 cup breadcrumbs
- 1 egg
- 1/4 cup BBQ sauce
- Salt, pepper
- Buns, toppings

Instructions:

1. Mix all ingredients and form 4 patties.
2. Grill over medium heat 5–6 minutes per side.
3. Serve on buns with extra BBQ sauce and desired toppings.

Grilled Halloumi Cheese

Ingredients:

- 8 oz halloumi cheese, sliced
- 1 tbsp olive oil
- Lemon wedges (optional)

Instructions:

1. Preheat grill to medium-high.
2. Lightly oil cheese slices.
3. Grill 2–3 minutes per side until golden grill marks appear.
4. Serve warm with lemon.

BBQ Pork Tenderloin

Ingredients:

- 1–1.5 lb pork tenderloin
- Salt, pepper, garlic powder
- 1/2 cup BBQ sauce

Instructions:

1. Preheat grill to medium.
2. Season pork and grill 15–20 minutes, turning occasionally.
3. Brush with BBQ sauce in the last 5 minutes.
4. Rest 5–10 minutes before slicing.

Grilled Peach Halves

Ingredients:

- 4 ripe peaches, halved and pitted
- 1 tbsp olive oil or melted butter
- Optional: honey, cinnamon

Instructions:

1. Brush peach halves with oil or butter.
2. Grill cut-side down over medium heat for 3–4 minutes.
3. Drizzle with honey and sprinkle cinnamon, if desired.

BBQ Glazed Meatloaf

Ingredients:

- 1 lb ground beef
- 1/2 cup breadcrumbs
- 1 egg
- 1/4 cup onion, finely chopped
- 1/2 cup BBQ sauce (divided)

Instructions:

1. Mix beef, breadcrumbs, egg, onion, and 1/4 cup BBQ sauce.
2. Shape into loaf and place in grill-safe foil pan.
3. Grill over indirect heat for 35–40 minutes.
4. Brush with remaining BBQ sauce in last 10 minutes.

Grilled Romaine Salad

Ingredients:

- 2 heads romaine, halved lengthwise
- 1 tbsp olive oil
- Salt and pepper
- Optional toppings: Parmesan, balsamic glaze

Instructions:

1. Brush romaine halves with olive oil, season lightly.
2. Grill cut-side down for 1–2 minutes.
3. Top with Parmesan or drizzle of balsamic.

BBQ Bratwursts

Ingredients:

- 5–6 bratwurst sausages
- 5–6 buns
- Optional: sauerkraut, mustard, onions

Instructions:

1. Grill brats over medium heat for 15–20 minutes, turning often.
2. Optionally toast buns on grill.
3. Serve brats with your favorite toppings.

Grilled Swordfish Steaks

Ingredients:

- 2 swordfish steaks (6 oz each)
- 1 tbsp olive oil
- Salt, pepper, lemon juice

Instructions:

1. Brush steaks with oil and season.
2. Grill over medium-high heat 4–5 minutes per side.
3. Drizzle with lemon juice before serving.

BBQ Cauliflower Steaks

Ingredients:

- 1 large head cauliflower
- 2 tbsp olive oil
- Salt, pepper, garlic powder
- 1/2 cup BBQ sauce

Instructions:

1. Slice cauliflower into 3/4" steaks.
2. Brush with oil and seasonings.
3. Grill over medium heat 5–6 minutes per side.
4. Brush with BBQ sauce during last few minutes.

Grilled Bacon-Wrapped Asparagus

Ingredients:

- 1 bunch asparagus, trimmed
- 8 slices bacon
- Toothpicks (optional)

Instructions:

1. Wrap 3–4 spears per bacon slice, secure with toothpicks.
2. Grill over medium heat for 8–10 minutes, turning occasionally, until bacon is crisp.
3. Serve hot.

BBQ Glazed Tofu Skewers

Ingredients:

- 1 block extra-firm tofu, pressed and cubed
- 1/2 cup BBQ sauce
- 1 tbsp olive oil
- Salt and pepper to taste
- Skewers (soaked if wooden)

Instructions:

1. Toss tofu cubes in olive oil, salt, pepper, and BBQ sauce.
2. Thread onto skewers.
3. Grill over medium heat, 8–10 minutes, turning occasionally and basting with more sauce.
4. Serve hot.

Grilled Nachos

Ingredients:

- Tortilla chips
- 1 cup shredded cheese (cheddar or Mexican blend)
- 1/2 cup black beans
- 1/2 cup cooked meat (optional)
- Jalapeños, diced tomatoes, and green onions
- Foil pan or grill-safe tray

Instructions:

1. Layer chips, cheese, beans, and toppings in foil pan.
2. Place on grill, lid closed, for 5–7 minutes or until cheese melts.
3. Serve with salsa, sour cream, or guacamole.

Grilled Avocado Halves

Ingredients:

- 2 ripe avocados, halved and pitted
- Olive oil
- Salt and pepper
- Optional: lime juice, chopped cilantro

Instructions:

1. Brush cut sides with olive oil and season.
2. Grill cut-side down for 2–3 minutes until grill marks form.
3. Serve as-is or filled with salsa or shrimp salad.

BBQ Chicken Pizza

Ingredients:

- 1 pizza crust (pre-cooked or naan)
- 1/2 cup BBQ sauce
- 1 cup cooked, shredded chicken
- 1 cup mozzarella cheese
- Red onion slices and cilantro (optional)

Instructions:

1. Spread BBQ sauce over crust, add chicken, cheese, and toppings.
2. Grill over indirect heat, lid closed, for 8–10 minutes or until cheese is bubbly.
3. Slice and serve.

Grilled Stuffed Peppers

Ingredients:

- 4 bell peppers, halved and seeded
- 1 cup cooked rice or cauliflower rice
- 1/2 cup cooked ground meat or beans
- 1/2 cup shredded cheese
- Spices to taste

Instructions:

1. Mix filling ingredients and spoon into pepper halves.
2. Grill over indirect heat for 10–15 minutes until peppers are tender.
3. Top with more cheese and grill 2 more minutes to melt.

BBQ Chicken Quesadillas

Ingredients:

- 2 large tortillas
- 1/2 cup shredded cooked chicken
- 1/4 cup BBQ sauce
- 1 cup shredded cheese
- Optional: red onion, cilantro

Instructions:

1. Mix chicken with BBQ sauce.
2. Place on half of tortilla with cheese and toppings; fold over.
3. Grill 2–3 minutes per side until crispy and golden.
4. Slice and serve.

Grilled Scallops

Ingredients:

- 1 lb sea scallops
- 1 tbsp olive oil
- Salt, pepper, garlic powder
- Lemon wedges

Instructions:

1. Pat scallops dry, toss in oil and seasoning.
2. Grill over high heat for 2–3 minutes per side until opaque.
3. Serve with lemon.

BBQ Sweet Potato Slices

Ingredients:

- 2 large sweet potatoes, sliced into 1/4" rounds
- 1 tbsp olive oil
- Salt, pepper, paprika
- 1/4 cup BBQ sauce (optional)

Instructions:

1. Toss slices in oil and seasonings.
2. Grill over medium heat for 4–5 minutes per side.
3. Brush with BBQ sauce in final minute if desired.

Grilled Cornbread

Ingredients:

- 1 pan of baked cornbread, cut into squares
- Butter for brushing

Instructions:

1. Lightly butter cornbread slices.
2. Grill over medium heat for 1–2 minutes per side until grill marks appear.
3. Serve warm.

BBQ Cheeseburgers

Ingredients:

- 1 lb ground beef (80/20)
- Salt and pepper
- 4 hamburger buns
- 4 slices cheese (cheddar, American, etc.)
- BBQ sauce
- Lettuce, tomato, and pickles (optional)

Instructions:

1. Form beef into 4 patties and season with salt and pepper.
2. Grill over medium-high heat for 4–5 minutes per side.
3. Add cheese during the last minute of grilling.
4. Toast buns on the grill, then assemble with BBQ sauce and toppings.

Grilled Pineapple Chicken

Ingredients:

- 2 chicken breasts
- 1/2 cup pineapple juice
- 2 tbsp soy sauce
- 1 tbsp olive oil
- 1 tbsp honey
- Salt and pepper
- 1 cup fresh pineapple, sliced

Instructions:

1. Marinate chicken in pineapple juice, soy sauce, olive oil, honey, salt, and pepper for at least 30 minutes.
2. Grill chicken for 6–7 minutes per side.
3. Grill pineapple slices for 2–3 minutes per side.
4. Serve chicken topped with grilled pineapple.

BBQ Duck Breasts

Ingredients:

- 2 duck breasts
- Salt and pepper
- 1/4 cup BBQ sauce
- 1 tbsp olive oil

Instructions:

1. Score the duck skin and season with salt and pepper.
2. Grill over medium heat, skin-side down, for 6–8 minutes.
3. Flip and grill for another 4–5 minutes until desired doneness.
4. Brush with BBQ sauce during the last minute.
5. Let rest before slicing.

Grilled Stuffed Mushrooms

Ingredients:

- 12 large mushrooms, stems removed
- 1/2 cup cream cheese, softened
- 1/4 cup grated Parmesan
- 1/4 cup breadcrumbs
- 2 tbsp garlic, minced
- 1 tbsp olive oil
- Salt and pepper

Instructions:

1. Mix cream cheese, Parmesan, breadcrumbs, garlic, olive oil, salt, and pepper.
2. Stuff mushroom caps with the mixture.
3. Grill over medium heat for 6–8 minutes, until mushrooms are tender.

BBQ Glazed Tempeh

Ingredients:

- 1 block tempeh, sliced into 1/2" strips
- 1/2 cup BBQ sauce
- 1 tbsp olive oil
- Salt and pepper

Instructions:

1. Brush tempeh slices with olive oil, salt, and pepper.
2. Grill over medium heat for 3–4 minutes per side.
3. Brush with BBQ sauce during the last minute of grilling.
4. Serve with extra sauce.

Grilled Garlic Bread

Ingredients:

- 1 loaf French or Italian bread, sliced
- 4 tbsp butter, softened
- 2 cloves garlic, minced
- 1 tbsp parsley, chopped
- Salt to taste

Instructions:

1. Mix butter, garlic, parsley, and salt.
2. Spread mixture on each bread slice.
3. Grill over medium heat for 1–2 minutes per side until golden and crispy.

www.ingramcontent.com/pod-product-compliance
Lightning Source LLC
LaVergne TN
LVHW081323060526
838201LV00055B/2425